YOUR KNOWLEDGE HAS VALUE

Harry Körner

Michael Moore. A Rebel and his Counter-Rebels

GRIN Verlag

Bibliografische Information der Deutschen Nationalbibliothek:

Die Deutsche Bibliothek verzeichnet diese Publikation in der Deutschen National-
bibliografie; detaillierte bibliografische Daten sind im Internet über http://dnb.d-
nb.de/ abrufbar.

Imprint:

Copyright © 2005 GRIN Verlag GmbH
Druck und Bindung: Books on Demand GmbH, Norderstedt Germany
ISBN: 978-3-656-69538-7

This book at GRIN:

http://www.grin.com/en/e-book/232775/michael-moore-a-rebel-and-his-counter-
rebels

GRIN - Your knowledge has value

Der GRIN Verlag publiziert seit 1998 wissenschaftliche Arbeiten von Studenten, Hochschullehrern und anderen Akademikern als eBook und gedrucktes Buch. Die Verlagswebsite www.grin.com ist die ideale Plattform zur Veröffentlichung von Hausarbeiten, Abschlussarbeiten, wissenschaftlichen Aufsätzen, Dissertationen und Fachbüchern.

Visit us on the internet:

http://www.grin.com/

http://www.facebook.com/grincom

http://www.twitter.com/grin_com

1

Index

1. Introduction   p. 2

2. Michael Moore – a short biography   p. 2

3. Michael Moore and his two most recent outputs   p. 3

3.1. Dude, Where's My Country?   p. 4

3.1.1. Plot   p. 4

3.1.2. Author's intention and how it is expressed   p. 8

3.2. Fahrenheit 9/11   p. 8

3.2.1. Plot   p. 8

3.2.2. Author's intention and how it is expressed   p. 10

3.2.3. Some supposed attempts of deception   p. 12

3.2.4. Distribution problems   p. 13

4. Actions of his opponents   p. 15

4.1. Celsius 41.11   p. 15

4.2. Michael Moore Is A Big Fat Stupid White Man   p. 16

4.3. Internet offers   p. 17

5. Personal statement   p. 17

6. Bibliography   p. 18

1. Introduction

When on November 2nd in the year 2004 the world's single left super-power's citizens went to choose between incumbent George W. Bush and his challenger John F. Kerry to become the nation's next president, the whole planet glanced excitedly at their TV in order to be informed as soon as possible about whom of the two would be the one to lead the United States of America in the forthcoming four years. Too much had been happening between 2000 and 2004, during the first period of the Bush administration in power. Events like the terror attacks on September 11th 2001, the resultant Afghanistan war and so-called war on terror and of course – most importantly – the invasion of Iraq which began in march 2003 and was suspected not to be waged due to the existence of Saddam's mysterious "weapons of mass destruction", but much more likely because of the country's extensive oil fields, had been changing the world's political consciousness and especially the view towards a western civilization that did not seem to stand for peace-keeping or democracy any more, as it was seen almost a whole century ago, but as a Goliath that was trying to raise a hegemony just to be able to fulfill his wishes no matter which non-allied country or people with a different culture suffered from this.

Yet it was not only abroad that vast forms of protest began to form themselves, but also in the U.S. One of this movement's most polarizing phenomenons is meanwhile world-widely known and had not least co-motivated these developments in Europe and particularly in Germany: leftist writer, director and polemic Michael Moore.

As a vehement critic of his government's policy, this man specially published a book and a film in the wider pre-election phase only with the goal of removing Bush from his presidency. This agitator, these two outputs and how his opponents try to prevent him from spreading his message shall be dealt with on the following pages.

2. Michael Moore – a short biography[1]

Born in 1954 in a suburb of Flint, Michigan, called Davison, Moore grew up under the impression of his father and grandfather both working at General Motors; his mother was a secretary. An early touch with politics was attained through his uncle, who was one of the founders of the United Automobile Workers labor union and was part of the

---

[1] cp. Wikipedia: MM

famous Sitdown strike held against General Motors by its workers. Since he was born into a catholic family, he attended a Diocesan seminary when he was 14, afterwards went on to Davison High School and graduated in 1972. In the same year he made his first kind of active political experience when he got elected for a seat on the Davison school board which aimed the eventually successful firing of the school's principal and vice principal. "Also of note is that Michael Moore is an Eagle Scout, the highest rank in Boy Scouting. For his Eagle Project, he filmed a documentary pointing out various safety hazards and issues within his community."[2] At the age of 22 Michael Moore founded an alternative weekly magazine, the Flint Voice, which was renamed in Michigan Voice after a short while. In 1986 he moved to California to work as an editor at political magazine Mother Jones. At the same time the Michigan Voice closed down. After five months he was fired because of his disapproval of an article about the Sandinista government in Nicaragua which he thought to be "unfairly critical"[3]. As a result of being fired Moore received $58,000 from an out-of-court settlement after having "sued for wrongful dismissal"[4]. The money was used to produce his first mainstream trademark-Moore-style award-winning documentary, Roger And Me.

Michael Moore is married to 46-year old Kathleen Glynn. Their daughter Natalie was born in 1981.

Other known works by him are the films The Big One (1997) and the Oscar-winning anti-gun documentary Bowling For Columbine (2002) and his two predecessor-books Downsize This! (1996) and the famous number one best-seller Stupid White Men (2001). For television he created the two series TV Nation and The Awful Truth which both won an Emmy.

3. Michael Moore and his two most recent outputs

As said in the introduction, Moore published two works directly aiming to get Bush out of power in the 2004 presidential election: in October 2003 his book Dude, Where's My Country? reached the bookstores and in 2004 his documentary Fahrenheit 9/11 had general release in the United States and Canada on June 25th, just four months and a week before the election.

---

[2] Wikipedia: MM
[3] Wikipedia: MM
[4] Wikipedia: MM

3.1. Dude, Where's My Country?[5]

3.1.1. Plot

The book is structured in eleven main chapters, lead by an introduction and followed by a reference to notes and sources, acknowledgments and a short section about the author. It is continuously held in a satiric tone which starts even before the table of contents on the very first page with an ironic text headlined by "APPROVED"[6] where Moore lets "Tom Ridge, Secretary of the Homeland [and] George W. Bush, Commander in Chief of the Fatherland"[7] ensure that "[t]his book has been approved by the Department of Homeland Security. It contains no seditious acts or acts of treason. Each word has been examined and analyzed by a team of terrorism experts to insure that it gives neither aid nor comfort to The Enemy."[8] Hereby the author makes an allusion to the USA Patriot Act that has been passed by the Bush administration after the attacks of September 11th in order to complicate it for potential terrorists to enter the country or live there as so-called sleepers until committing an assault.

The first chapter is called "7 Questions for George of Arabia"[9] and consequently consists of seven questions (rather claims) concerning the relationship between the Bushes and the bin Laden family, their connection to the Saudi royal family, a presumption of Saudi Arabia being in charge of September 11th instead of bin Laden and the Taliban, the statement that members of the bin Laden family were flown out of the U.S. shortly after the attacks without having been investigated by the FBI, a question why the Second Amendment is also valid for potential evildoers, the question whether George W. Bush knew that when he was "(…) governor of Texas, the Taliban travelled to Texas to meet with your oil and gas company friends"[10] and finally what the look on the president's face was when he heard of the terror assaults while reading to an elementary class in Sarasota, Florida.

"Home of the Whopper" is chapter two's ajar-at-a big fast food company-title in which ten different menu names stand for ten lies told by Bush and his crew in the fore field of the Iraq war, e.g., " #3 Whopper with Bacon: 'Iraq has ties to Osama bin Laden and al

---

[5] cp. DwimC 2003
[6] DwimC 2003, very first page
[7] DwimC 2003, very first page
[8] DwimC 2003, very first page
[9] DwimC 2003, p. 1
[10] DwimC 2003, p. 26

Qaeda!'"[11] Or "#10 Triple Whopper, Biggie Size: 'We didn't lie. And we're not lying now to cover up the lies we told you before.'"[12] Each of these lies is contradicted by Moore with reference to independent media sources or historical background knowledge.

In the third chapter "Oil's Well That Ends Well"[13] the author narrates a fictional dream in which he has had a conversation with his great-grand-daughter, Anne Coulter Moore, in the year 2054. The little girl asks him about how our civilization functioned and her great-grandfather tells her how much easier it was then to make a living because there was still enough oil and a working environment around. But since no one cared about the oil an the environment, between 2005 and 2015 living conditions got worse and even more wars about natural resources were fought so that a big dying among humankind took place and only few managed to survive. Although it is all written in a funny style with some jokes here and there a flashback is created that shall be an impulse to think about current habits.

The next chapter is: "The United States of *BOO!*"[14] It deals with the safety hysteria developed by the government: "According to the Bush administration, and the stories they have planted in the media, the terrorists are *everywhere*. Each day seems to bring a new warning. A new alert! *A new threat!*"[15] Furthermore, Moore encounters a few incidents which were only possible because of this policy, for example when "(...) an alert Oklahoma pump attendant called authorities when a group pulled in with two vans and an equipment truck. Within minutes, police and FBI had surrounded, with guns drawn, the rock band Godspeed You! Black Emperor. Released after hours of questioning, singer Efrim Menuck told *Seattle Weekly*, 'We're just lucky we're nice white kids from Canada.'"[16]

Chapter 5 is named, "How to Stop Terrorism? Stop Being Terrorists!"[17] Here Michael Moore tells the reader to listen to his 18-points-program for homeland security instead of Bush's one, containing sarcastic advice like, "**4. When attempting to prop up a Latin American dictator, try to do it without killing too many nuns or archbishops**"[18], "**5. When attempting to assassinate the president of Cuba, make**

---

[11] DwimC 2003, p. 53
[12] DwimC 2003, p. 81
[13] DwimC 2003, p. 85
[14] DwimC 2003, p. 95
[15] DwimC 2003, p. 98
[16] DwimC 2003, p. 99
[17] DwimC 2003, p. 119
[18] DwimC 2003, p. 120

sure you get the right kind of exploding cigars"[19] or "**17. Start bombing the hell out of people with WHITE skin**"[20] etc.

In "Jesus W. Christ"[21], the sixth chapter, the author pretends to be God and makes fun of Bush's displayed Christianity by quoting some of his sentences concerning faith. He gives orders by summing up a few Ten-Commandment-like phrases, "6. (…) My little-known Eleventh Commandment? Keep your religious convictions to your own damn selves."[22]

Within chapter seven, "Horatio Alger Must Die"[23], Moore criticises the mentality of U.S. CEOs, whom he depicts as greedy "corporate mujahedeen"[24]. He suggests them to exploit the country and its citizens and read out one day

> "(…) the Declaration of the Corporate States of America.
>
> 'We hold these truths to be self-evident: that all men and women and their underaged children are created equally to serve the Corporation, to provide its labor without question, to accept whatever remuneration without complaint, and to consume its products without thought. In turn, the Corporation will provide for the common good, secure the defense of the nation, and receive the bulk of the taxes taken from the people…'"[25]

Two "drugs"[26] are given to the people: "One of these drugs is called fear and the other is called Horatio Alger."[27] Fear is supposed to make the citizens trust in the corporations without questioning their measures; Horatio Alger is a synonym for the legendary American Dream. But Moore says that this dream will never become reality for the vast majority of Americans. According to him, not to be born to "their club"[28] means in almost every case staying out of it for the rest of the live. So, also the average man's naivety is outlined by the author.

---

[19] DwimC 2003, p. 121
[20] DwimC 2003, p. 126
[21] DwimC 2003, p. 129
[22] DwimC 2003, p. 134
[23] DwimC 2003, p. 137
[24] DwimC 2003, p. 137
[25] DwimC 2003, p. 138
[26] DwimC 2003, p. 138
[27] DwimC 2003, p. 138
[28] DwimC 2003, p. 141

The eighth chapter is called "Woo Hoo! I Got Me a Tax Cut!"[29] and consists of a letter
to George W. Bush written by Michael Moore as himself.

In this letter he criticises the president's fiscal policy (after all a \$350 billion tax cut[30])
as to be only in favour of the rich and leaving behind the poor respectively what ought
to be done for them by the ironically exaggerated thanking for the profit he – now due
to his successful works rich himself – gains additionally.

"A Liberal Paradise"[31] as the ninth chapter states that the U.S. is not such a conservative
place at all, but indeed full of liberal thinking persons. The only thing why
conservatives are so much louder is why the have to be – a minority that wants
implicitly to be heard. As for this, the author quotes some dictums spread by them via
the media, e.g.: "'WE NEED TO EXECUTE PEOPLE LIKE JOHN WALKER IN
ORDER TO PHYSICALLY INTIMIDATE LIBERALS, BY MAKING THEM
REALIZE THAT THEY CAN BE KILLED, TOO. OTHERWISE THEY WILL TURN
OUT TO BE OUTRIGHT TRAITORS!' –Ann Coulter"[32]

Chapter ten: "How to Talk to Your Conservative Brother-in-Law"[33] is started with the
imagination of a typical American family-situation. It is Thanksgiving dinner and there
is always some family member who comes to politics and has a different (which means
conservative) point of view. Based on this stereotyped situation Moore wants to teach
the reader how to deal with such a person and possibly manage to convince him or her
of the opposite by arguing quietly and honestly – which means giving up long kept but
finally false positions oneself.

The last chapter, "Bush Removal and Other Spring Cleaning Chores"[34], is, with a wink,
a bill of potential Bush-defeaters who could run for presidency in case the Democrats
would not find an appropriate candidate. According to the book, Moore's favourite
celebrity is definitely Oprah Winfrey, a famous talk master, which becomes clear in
sentences like the following: "(...) she will answer the call to lead us out of our national
misery. Oprah! Oprah! Oprah!"[35]

---

[29] DwimC 2003, p. 157
[30] DwimC 2003, p. 157
[31] DwimC 2003, p. 165
[32] in: DwimC 2003, p. 176
[33] DwimC 2003, p. 183
[34] DwimC 2003, p. 203
[35] Dwimc 2003, p. 209

3.1.2. Author's intention and how it is expressed

As already mentioned, the book was published in the wider pre-election phase.
Thus it becomes pretty obvious what it was meant for: the successful removal of incumbent George W. Bush from the presidency of the United States of America. In order to achieve this aim, Moore accuses Bush of several malfeasances like for instance hypocrisy ("Just go straight for the oil and cut out the bullshit about nation building or democracy."[36]), lobbyism ("Yes, when it comes to guns, finally the rights of foreigners count for something."[37]) and direct lying ("Maybe the reason Bush is still here is that he proved the old adage that if you tell a lie long enough and often enough, sooner or later it becomes the truth."[38]). But these are only a few of many explicit sentences in the text that make the author's mission unmistakably obvious. This book tries to attack and reveal to the ultimate degree. That, in the end, the intent would fail, Michael Moore does not have to project on himself because with this book he did almost anything one can do on a literally basis.

3.2. Fahrenheit 9/11

3.2.1. Plot[39]

In general, most of its content can be compared to the one of Dude, Where's My Country? Summed up, the film deals with the election four years ago, the terror attacks on September 11th, the invasion and occupation of Iraq and Bush's financial ties to Saudi Arabia respectively the bin Laden family. Some remaining scenes were the following ones:
At the beginning there is a short flashback onto the 2000 presidential election, when, according to Michael Moore, the fooling of the public was initiated by a relative of George W. Bush working at Fox News Channel, letting the anchorman say the Republicans won Florida. After this message was spread via television, all the other

---

[36] Dwimc 2003, p. 125
[37] Dwimc 2003, p. 25
[38] Dwimc 2003, p. 42
[39] cp. F 9/11

channels took over this claim, thus generating a broad "Bush-has-won"-feeling that could have had an effect on the counting process of still remaining votes.

Then Moore states that until the attacks of September 11th Bush had been on vacation for 42% of his incumbency, showing pictures of a busy golfing president.

The next remarkable scene is when Bush is reading a book to some elementary pupils in Florida, interrupted by a member of staff telling him that America is under attack. For the following long-lasting seven minutes the spectator sees a president of the United States of America who stares into the room with a perplex facial expression, doing absolutely nothing except for this and being calm. Of course, while sitting in front of the screen all the time in a full but totally quiet hall waiting for something to happen, this affects the spectator to think of George W. Bush as to be incapable and slow.

As for the Saudi/bin Laden-theme, for instance, Moore states that bin Laden family members were flown out of the U.S. just after the terror attacks without having been investigated by the FBI when nobody else was allowed to fly.

Or later in the film he presents a document from the time Bush served as an Air National Guard with a name (James Bath) of a former fellow on it, who later worked for the Saudis as a financial agent. This man helped channel Saudi- and bin Laden-money into Bush's faltering oil company called Arbusto. Furthermore, the author accuses the White House of deception by presenting an edited version of this document with the fellow's name censored out (accordingly Moore somehow managed to obtain an original version).

The movie's last part focuses on the Iraq-complex of themes (even if there were some scenes with war-injured soldiers in it before):

Firstly Moore questions the army's recruiting methods by accompanying two head hunters who mainly concentrate on young people coming from poorer areas respectively social backgrounds. They even promise a better chance for a musical career to a black Hip Hop-interested teenager by telling him that acts like Shaggy served their duty before becoming a pop star.

Later the film shows some cuttings from a business convention where corporate representatives are told about the possibilities for their business to make money through the Iraq war.

At another point in the film Moore rushes after Congressmen and –women going to work asking them to enlist their children for a mission to Iraq (according to Moore, only one Congressman's child serves in Iraq). As expected, he only gains pettish or furious answers, if they do not pass by without a word or even run away at once.

The very last segment concerning Iraq and of the film as a whole is about a mother, Lila Lipscomb, a woman from Flint, Michigan, who has turned from a convinced war supporter to an opponent after her son was sent to Iraq, telling her in his letters about the uselessness of it and finally dying in it. Now she wants to be heard in her pain and travels to Washington D.C. in order to protest in front of the White House, followed by Michael Moore and his camera. This part of the film definitely has the most moving effect on the spectator, showing a desperate mother with tears in her eyes and a shuttering voice standing alone face to face with the Oval Office.

3.2.2. Author's intention and how it is expressed[40]

When it was announced for the best picture, winning the Palme d'Or at the 2004 film festival in Cannes, chances seemed high – backed like this – of achieving Bush's removal from the White House; later it would be "approaching $150 in worldwide grosses"[41], thus being "a show business anomaly"[42]. Released just about four months prior to the presidential election, it was "less a movie than a major salvo in the presidential campaign"[43] as seen by an English newspaper. According to a New York Times article, "Michael Moore is not coy about his hopes for 'Fahrenheit 9/11,' his documentary attack on President Bush and the war in Iraq that opened in the United States on June 25. He wants it to be remembered as the first big-audience, election-year film that helped unseat a president."[44] But, in addition, it is asked whether, "(...) the film's depiction of Mr. Bush as a lazy and duplicitous leader, blinded by his family's financial ties to Arab moneymen and the Saudi Arabian royal family [is] true to fact?"[45] Yet Moore, in order to nip those questions in the bud, had let his production staff take "(...) no chances in checking and double-checking the film, knowing Bush supporters

---

[40] cp. Kehr 2004; Scott 2004; Patterson 2004; Shenon 2004; Brockes 2004; Kaffsack 2004
[41] Kehr 2004
[42] Scott 2004
[43] Patterson 2004
[44] Shenon 2004
[45] Shenon 2004

would pounce on factual mistakes."[46] He assures: "'Any attempts to libel me will be met by force.'"[47]

Indeed, to get Bush out of power, Moore seems to use anything, also pictures that are only good for creating a very subjective sentiment of dislike for him: "Mr. Moore makes extensive use of obscure footage from White House and network-news video archives, including scenes that capture President Bush at his least articulate."[48] For instance, as the New York Times says, "Mr. Bush's slow, hesitant reaction to the disastrous news has never been a secret. But seeing the actual footage, with the minutes ticking by, may prove more damaging to the White House than all the statistics in the world."[49]

Nevertheless, the (not accidentally last) part with Lila Lipscomp in it holds the movie's mainly striking scenes:

"It is two weeks since Fahrenheit 9/11, Michael Moore's polemic on the war in Iraq, was released in America, and in that time Lipscomb's voice has emerged as the film's most powerful."[50] The total change of a human life and the sad, depressive mood that can easily be felt by the spectator and also the ability to articulate this state of mind in a proper way make it "(...) hard to resist the testimony of 50-year-old Lipscomb, a mother from Flint, Michigan, who still flies a flag in her garden, but is down to three children and a handful or ruptured assumptions where other certainties used to be. The scenes in which she recounts the story of her son Michael's death have had cinema-goers sniffing into their sleeves."[51]

American jury-president and director himself, Quentin Tarantino ("'We thought this movie to be the best one we have seen.'"[52]), assured to journalists at Cannes that the price-giving was not politically motivated. However, this is hard to believe when you think of the post-electoral outcry of a big amount of Hollywood's stars and most of America's musicians, artists and intellectuals that all recommended this film.

---

[46] Shenon 2004
[47] in: Shenon 2004
[48] Shenon 2004
[49] Shenon 2004
[50] Brockes 2004
[51] Brockes 2004
[52] in: Kaffsack 2004

3.2.3. Some supposed attempts of deception[53]

For all what is already said about this film, as expected there are voices that try to weaken or disown its message.

For one, U.S.-American critic David Kopel made a list of 59 Deceits of which I will point out some that contradict parts of the plot-section:

- "2. Like all the other networks, Fox mistakenly said that Gore had won in Florida. The first network to retract the Florida mistake was CBS, not Fox."[54]

- "3. A 6-month study by a consortium of major newspapers shows that Bush would have won the Florida recount under any of the terms which Gore sought in his lawsuits."[55]

- "6. 'In his first eight months in office before September 11th, George W. Bush was on vacation, according to the Washington Post, forty-two percent of the time.' As the Washington Post reported, the figure includes weekends, and includes time in 'vacation locations' such as Camp David, where Bush was working – as when he met with Tony Blair."[56]

- "11. The Saudis left the U.S. only after air travel was opened for the general public."[57]

- "14. Contrary to what *Fahrenheit* claims, the September 11 Commission staff found that many Saudis were asked 'detailed questions' before being allowed to leave."[58]

- "16. James Bath did not invest bin Laden family money in Bush's energy company Arbusto. He invested his own money."[59]

- "17. Bath's name was blacked-out from an Alabama National Guard record released by the White House – as required by federal law, which prohibits the disclosure of health-related personal information."[60]

- "53. Moore claims that only one Congressman has a child in Iraq. Actually, two do. (Democratic Senator Tim Johnson of S.D., and Republican Rep. Duncan

---

[53] cp. Kopel 2004
[54] Kopel 2004, p. 1
[55] Kopel 2004, p. 1
[56] Kopel 2004, p. 1
[57] Kopel 2004, p. 1
[58] Kopel 2004, p. 1
[59] Kopel 2004, p. 2
[60] Kopel 2004, p. 2

Hunter of California.) Also, John Ashcroft has a son on a naval ship in the Persian Gulf."[61]

- "57. Moore calls Flint, Michigan, 'my hometown.' In fact, he grew up in Davison, a much wealthier and much whiter suburb."[62]

Whether facts like the last one are really necessary in a seriously led discussion lies in everyone's own discretion. But, of course, a politically motivated film should, despite all funny and polemic elements, stick to reality. It is hard to say who is right in this contrasting of two statements due to Michael Moore's affirmation of fact-checking. So, in the end you also have to deal with a third factor, your own feeling, which can lead into deception as well.

3.2.4. Distribution problems[63]

"Disney's Miramax division, headed by Bob and Harvey Weinstein, bankrolled the film, but Disney head Michael Eisner refused to release it, citing Disney's tradition as a 'nonpartisan company' – you know, the sort of nonpartisan company whose ABC Radio division gives a forum to conservative ideologues. The Moore camp points to the Florida-based Disney's need to do business in a state governed by the president's brother – and since the film is nearly as harsh about Saudi royals as about George Bush himself, isn't it suspicious that money from one of those royals, Prince Alwaleed bin Talal, is keeping the financially troubled EuroDisney afloat? Or is that another Michael Moore-style conspiracy theory? If, as some observers believe, Eisner's real motivation was to stick it to his archrival Harvey Weinstein, it backfired."[64]

This passage can be found in an issue of famous news magazine Newsweek in an article concerning the movie. Here are some more facts for general understanding:
Originally the idea was that Icon Productions (owned by Mel Gibson) distributes the movie, but later resigned "(…) citing image conflicts while claiming the decision to be

---

[61] Kopel 2004, p. 3
[62] Kopel 2004, p. 4
[63] cp. Gates 2004; Wikipedia: controversy; Ellis 2004
[64] Gates 2004, pp. 52-54

apolitical."[65] It was then taken by the Weinstein's Miramax, but in May 2004 its parent company, Disney, wanted to prevent them from releasing it, "(...) citing a contractual clause expressly permitting it to do so in such cases as a prohibitive budget or explicit movie rating"[66] and having advised Moore and Miramax in May 2003 that the permission would not be granted for the film's publishing being "counterproductive to the interests of the company"[67] (but, instead of this, liasons to Disney told him to finish his movie all the same, as Moore claims). According to a Disney executive, they would have been "'dragged into a highly charged partisan political battle'"[68] if releasing it, expecting negative influence on subjects such as tax breaks on Disney property in (by the president's brother Jeb Bush governed) Florida. In addition, "Disney also has financial ties to members of the Saudi royal family, who were represented unfavorably in the film."[69] Because of all those obscurities, the movie's distribution was organized first in many countries other than the USA. Eventually, "On May 28, 2004, after more than a week of talks, Disney announced that Miramax film studio founders Harvey and Bob Weinstein had personally acquired the rights to the documentary from Walt Disney Co., after Disney declined to distribute it."[70] Four weeks after that, the major rights were fully reverted to Lions Gate Films, "which in partnership with the Weinstein's newly-formed company Fellowship Adventure Group (...) and IFC Films acquired the film for domestic theatrical distribution (...)"[71] All the costs so far paid by Disney and the remaining ones were taken over by the Weinsteins.

Another, rather bizarre aspect belonging to the overall distribution theme, took place in the Middle East's region: "Meanwhile, in the United Arab Emirates, the film is being offered the kind of support it doesn't need. According to Screen International, the UAE-based distributor Front Row Entertainment has been contacted by organisations related to the [radical Islamic and anti-American] Hezbollah in Lebanon with offers of help."[72]

---

[65] Wikipedia: controversy
[66] Wikipedia: controversy
[67] Wikipedia: controversy
[68] in: Wikipedia: controversy
[69] Wikipedia: controversy
[70] Wikipedia: controversy
[71] Wikipedia: controversy
[72] Ellis 2004

4. Actions of his opponents

Michael Moore being a polarizing phenomenon, there is of course a perceptible opposition to his views and the way he makes them popular. And, of course again, this opposition wants to be as successful as he is respectively even more, thus it tries to beat him with his very own methods; agitation with the help of film, literature and internet sites.

4.1. Celsius 41.11[73]

The New York Time's final statement on the anti-Moore film goes like this: "The filmmakers state that the title 'Celsius 41.11' represents 'the temperature at which the brain begins to die.' It's unclear if they intend for the title to represent what happens when you watch Mr Moore's film or their own, or whether it's simply some sort of elegant and pointed self-diagnosis."[74] Referring to the Washington Post, "there's really nothing more here than you can find watching dreadful political advertisements and dreadful political talk shows. You can get all that on cable television for a low monthly fee. Why pay extra for 'Celsius 41.11'?"[75]

This film by Lionel Chetwynd, Ted Steinberg (producers) and Kevin Knoblock (director) starts with a balladeer singing an anti-Kerry song as the World Trade Center is hit by a plane. The resultant WTC's tumbling is repeated a few times. It continues with a montage showing Saddam together with the plane-hijackers, followed by "some dead Kurds, a grisly amputation, Howard Dean doing his famous Iowa scream, Al Gore, Ted Kennedy, an Afghan woman's head being blown off in an execution, and some stirring words from President Bush."[76] Furthermore, there are some personalities of "American punditry"[77] uttering their opinion on current events. One of them, terrorism expert Mansoor Ijaz, "(...) delivers blunt opinions like the Arab world 'only understands strength' and expounds on the 'absolute nonsense' of the Clinton administration."[78] In the reviewing New York Times article which is quoted from in this

---

[73] cp. Dargis 2004; Kennicott 2004
[74] Dargis 2004
[75] Kennicott 2004
[76] Kennicott 2004
[77] Kennicott 2004
[78] Dargis 2004

Facharbeit, it is said that Ijaz is a nuclear scientist and chairman of an investment firm oil-dealing with governments of the Middle East. He is also supposed to having been interested in deals with Sudan, nowadays assumed to support terrorism by the State Department.

According to the article, Citizens United produced the film in order "'to refute the propaganda in Michael Moore's Fahrenheit 9/11.'"[79] Yet with its dullness, laziness inconsistency[80] and the "sloppy cut-and-paste strategy"[81] Moore is hardly to defeat. (Besides this one there were the films Fahrenhype 9/11 and Michael Moore Hates America that had the same general purpose.)

4.2. Michael Moore Is A Big Fat Stupid White Man[82]

The title of this book by David T. Hardy and Jason Clarke is put together out of Moore's Stupid White Men and Al Franken's Rush Limbaugh Is A Big Fat Idiot And Other Observations where they, among other things "compare Michael Moore to Hitler and the Egyptian mastermind of Islamic terror, Sayid Qutb."[83] As they conclude, "(…) Michael Moore firstly represents an anachronistic form of the left that at the latest was put on file of history with the fall of the Berlin Wall, and secondly merciless submits truth to his rhetoric."[84]

The two authors "disclose how the radical magazine Mother Jones fired the 'arbitrary' and 'suspicious' Moore; how he started his feud with his replacement, David Talbot, (…); how Ralph Nader's organization fired Moore; how he attacked Pauline Kael, Harlan Jacobson and other prominent critics who exposed the deceits of his schlockumentaries; how he lost a lawsuit for betraying fellow lefty activist Larry Stecco in 'Roger & Me,' etc."[85] In addition, howlers in his best-selling books Stupid White Men and Dude, Where's My Country? and his films Bowling For Columbine and Fahrenheit 9/11 are presented.

---

[79] in: Dargis 2004
[80] Kennicott 2004
[81] Dargis 2004
[82] cp. Kreye 2004; NewsMax 2004
[83] Kreye 2004
[84] Kreye 2004
[85] NewsMax 2004

4.3. Internet offers[86]

David T. Hardy and Jason Clarke did not just write a book confronting Moore and his work, but also the both of them have "websites that exclusively deal with the theme Michael Moore: mooreexposed.com and moorelies.com."[87]

On these sites, the user finds critical analyses of his works, so-called blogs where one can read daily news uploaded by the particular webmaster or even write some own statements or questions that again can be answered by the webmaster or other surfers who blog and, of course, a lot of links to other webpages with like-minded contents, for example moorewatch.com, bowlingfortruth.com or centigrade911.com.[88]

5. Personal statement

Principally, in my opinion criticism and free speech should always be taken for granted – looking back on this piece of writing – whether for Michael Moore or people with a different political attitude. But never mind what and how one thinks of him, his point of view and how it is revealed by him, for a lively and widely noticed general political discussion he is absolutely necessary in a time when high percentages of young adults tend to be apolitical and indifferent towards politics – with his behaviour, his outward appearance and ways of using modern media being the impulse for many of them to even start their very first interest in public affairs.

As for me, meanwhile knowing of him and his methodology a bit better (thus dealing with it in a more sensible kind), I was sometimes annoyed by his obvious polemic, but on the other hand it also helps you getting through a book so that you keep its content when the reading is done.

In a globalized world with the growing influence of the only one super-power United States of America, Michael Moore's efforts help making people more attentive for what is happening on a wider horizon, what is in my opinion – especially with a person minded like current president George W. Busch – essential for the keeping of a prevalent peaceful world.

---

[86] cp. Kreye 2004; mooreexposed.com; moorelies.com
[87] Kreye 2004
[88] mooreexposed.com; moorelies.com

6. Bibliography

1. Moore, M.: Dude, Where Is My Country?
   New York, 2003 (DwimC 2003)
2. Gates, D.: Agent Provocateur.
   In: Newsweek 2004, no. 26, p. 52-55 (Gates 2004)
3. Kaffsack, H.-J.: Verkleidetes Wahlkampfpamphlet.
   In: Fränkischer Sonntag, Jul 31, 2004, p. 8 (Kaffsack 2004)
4. Shenon, P.: Michael Moore Is Ready to Defend His Incendiary Movie.
   In: Süddeutsche Zeitung (New York Times), Jun 28, 2004, p. 14 (Shenon 2004)
5. Kreye, A.: Dumm und fett.
   In: Süddeutsche Zeitung, Jul 30, 2004, p. 13 (Kreye 2004)
6. Scott, A. O.: A New Market For Bravehearts?
   In: New York Times, Jul 11, 2004, p. 19 (Scott 2004)
7. Kehr, D.: Revisiting The Road To Iraq War, Step by Step.
   In: New York Times, Aug 20, 2004, p. 6 (Kehr 2004)
8. Dargis, M.: Lowering the Subtlety Of Political Discourse.
   In: New York Times, Oct 22, 2004, p. 1 (Dargis 2004)
9. Kennicott, P.: "Celsius 41.11" Generates Heat but No New Light.
   In: Washington Post, Oct 22, 2004, p. 5 (Kennicott 2004)
10. Ellis, S.: Fahrenheit 9/11 gets help offer from Hezbollah.
    In: Guardian, Jun 17, 2004, p. 14 (Ellis 2004)
11. Brockes, E.: The lie that killed my son.
    In: Guardian, Jul 8, 2004, p. 10 (Brockes 2004)
12. Patterson, J.: John Patterson joins the queue to see if Michael Moore's latest can
    bring down the house, or even the White House.
    In: Guardian, Jul 10, 2004, p. 15 (Patterson 2004)
13. Wikipedia: Early life.
    http://en.wikipedia.org/wiki/Michael_Moore (last viewed 22.01.2005 – 19:00)
    (Wikipedia: MM)
14. Wikipedia: Release controversy.
    http://en.wikipedia.org/wiki/Fahrenheit_9/11_controversy (last viewed 23.01.2005 -
    11:00)
    (Wikipedia: controversy)

15. Kopel, D.: Fifty-nine Deceits in Fahrenheit 911.
    http://www.liberalismus.at/Texte/59Deceits.pdf (last viewed 27.12.2004 – 15:00)
    (Kopel 2004)

16. NewsMax.com: Michael Moore Is A Big Fat Stupid White Man.
    http://www.newsmax.com/archives/articles/2004/6/23/165945.shtml (last viewed
    23.01.2005 – 15:00)
    (NewsMax 2004)

17. Moore, M.: Fahrenheit 9/11 – The temperature where freedom burns!
    published by Lions Gate Films; generally released in the U.S. on Jun 25, 2004
    (F 9/11)

18. The two pictures (in order of appearance):
    - http://new.bbc.co.uk/media/images/38262000//jpg/_38262768_michael_moore15
      0ap.jpg (downloaded 15.01.2005 – 16:45); Michael Moore
    - http://arts.telegraph.co.uk/arts/graphics/2004/07/07/bfwein.jpg (downloaded
      15.01.2005 – 16:45); Bob and Harvey Weinstein